BAD BLESSINGS

BAD BLESSINGS

Poems & Images of the Texan Persuasion

BARBARA BRANNON

BOLDFACE BOOKS · TEXAS

Bad Blessings: Poems & Images of the Texan Persuasion
© 2022 Barbara Brannon

BOLDFACE BOOKS · TEXAS
978-1-935619-49-9

"Hundredth Meridian" was among the hundred-word poems chosen for *Weaving the Terrain: Southwestern Poems*, ed. David Meischen and Scott Wiggerman (Poetry of the American Southwest, No. 3; Dos Gatos Press, 2017), and set to music when performed at its debut in Austin, Texas.

"Fourteen" was a Top Four winner in the 2021 Maria W. Faust Sonnet Contest and published in its anthology of that year.

"The rock chip," a 2016 Ron Rash Award for Poetry finalist, was published in *Broad River Review*, 2017.

More works by the author:
ww.barbarabrannon.com

CONTENTS

Preface Writing and the Western Experience............. 7

ABOUT
Metapoesis.. 13

ALONG
The slow road to Flomot............................... 16
Hundredth Meridian.................................... 21
The rock chip 23
Easter Comes to Tom Green County 24
Texas 86, Late October 26

AGO
The Finney Gin.. 30
Fourteen.. 32
Posted.. 34
Half-mown 36
Assisted Living 40

AWAY
Azujelos.. 45
Sextet.. 47
Prepare... 48
Evicted 50

ABOVE
Got to Find a Way Back Down 54
A penny on tails, and no one to give it to 56
A Wish.. 59
Bad Blessings... 60
Last and Final 63

Tex Randall readied for restoration, Canyon, January 2016

PREFACE
Writing and the Western Experience

I DIDN'T BECOME A RESIDENT of the Western U.S. due to inclination or desire, but by a roundabout route. My move west was due not to aspiration, but to accident and need. I was a come-here Texan, not a from-here one.

And so it was with my writing.

I wasn't one of those Texans who jauntily claimed she *got here as quick as she could,* either. I was a daughter of the Deep South, and it took a while for me to fall in love with the Lone Star State. Not only did I have to work at getting over the color green, as that "dean of Western writers" Wallace Stegner put it, I had to search hard for any scrap of my new country that might resonate.

I was not a horsewoman. Not a farmer, not a farmer's wife. Not an appreciator of brisket and beans. Not a fan of country and western music.

My stories and poems and history essays were almost exclusively set in the Eastern time zone. I'd grown up ten miles from Tara, that fictional seat of *Gone with the Wind* and the set of its real-life movie, and had traveled almost exclusively on the Eastern seaboard.

But then I removed from a coastal city with both white-sand beach and moss-draped river to the distaff side of the hundredth meridian.

I came to flat, dusty West Texas lacking the advantages of fourth- and seventh-grade state history. Without having visited the Alamo or the Astrodome. Without appreciating the differences between saguaro and prickly pear, steer and heifer, felt and straw. Caliche, dugout, pearl-snap, playa, prairie dog, pumpjack, remuda—all were new terms in my lexicon.

I showed up to my first-ever National Cowboy Symposium representing my new bosses, Texas Tech University Press, at the outset of a fall semester, in the *dry* heat of a summer that would linger till Thanksgiving. My new Justin ropers didn't keep me from feeling conspicuously out of place among the esteemed historians, novelists, storytellers, crafters, artists, performers. And cowboy poets. *Cowboy poetry?* I hadn't known it was a genre.

But I was swiftly introduced to legends like Red Steagall and Elmer Kelton. Photographers like Wyman Meinzer and Ann Taylor. Guardians of Comanche culture like Juanita Pahdopony and Harry Mithlo and Bruce Parker. Reenactors like Henry Crawford and Bob Bluthardt. Fiddle champions, chuck-wagon cooks, rodeo queens, saddle makers, cow callers, songwriters—what a feast of the West it was! I set out to better appreciate its every strange new offering, and I couldn't have picked a richer learning environment.

Reading Texas and the West was a necessity of my job. Western history and natural history, art and culture, fiction and poetry became my daily staples, and because I had not learned these as a student I soaked them up now. I had to work at it.

That's not to say I didn't resist; I continued to hold the East superior, and to gravitate back "home" as often as I could. I struggled with the divide.

My moment of reconciliation came like a Damascus-road conversion.

Driving back to Lubbock solo one Sunday from a conference in Albuquerque, I'd been wrestling with the storyline of a manuscript I was editing, a novel (yes, this is true:) whose Texas protagonist resists returning to her roots. The clincher of the plot came unbidden to me in a curbside café over tacos and a Dr Pepper. The rest of the way across

New Mexico, from mountains to mesas to the Llano Estacado (which by then I knew to pronounce *yah*-noh) I worked out the details in my mind and scribbled them in my Moleskine. By the time I reached home I'd made my peace with Texas.

There was no turning back. I was all in, as I'd heard poker cronies say.

The apprenticeship in Western letters had clicked, for having immersed myself in the masters as a matter of survival, I'd begun to appreciate a few things natives came by naturally.

The West is aspirational. We're drawn to follow the sun. The strongest pull is westward, across the meridian and beyond, toward the frontier of our imagination.

The West is resolute. No one, whether indigenous or arrival, can survive without determination in these open, arid, and rugged places.

The West is inventive. Conquering the unknown takes ingenuity in endeavors of all kinds.

The West is both old and new. The romance of the old West is a touchstone that invites fresh discovery and interpretation.

The West is worthy as story and setting. I came here as a stranger, tentative, uncertain I could stake a place in it. Now I've claimed it.

The poems in this collection spring from the "bad blessing" of leaving a beloved homeplace back East—then unexpectedly finding a voice in the West. Over my decades in Texas I've crafted cowboy poems and composed country tunes. Learned to enjoy Western swing. Finished that first novel and written more. Sunk my teeth into Texas history. Driven lots of farm-to-market roads. Visited the Alamo.

These poems represent a range of verse inspired by the experience. Enjoy them with a salt-rimmed margarita, bootheels perched on the porch rail as you face the setting sun.

Spur, Thanksgiving 2022

Blanco Canyon, March 2021

ABOUT

Metapoesis

A poem is
a puzzle set
in the frame of
its own making

Flomot, August 2014

ALONG

Flomot, December morning, 2016

The slow road to Flomot

—not the way you want to go
if promptness matters—
will get you there
if there is the middle
of nowhere. The townsite
itself straddling the county line
like the spine of the wild hog
you know lurks rooting behind
that row of trees, the yellow
center stripe your guide,
the name a portmanteau you might
have packed if you'd boarded
the last stage arriving
here a century ago.

Some lanes were never made to race.
One mile stretch taut and straight
as a roper might drag a steer,
thin as wire across a fret,
suddenly crooks an elbow
to embrace the section line—
from there it's got more curves
than a star hurler
on the Motley team or
the top twirler from Floyd.
Twisting up the rise beside
the Haystack Ranch, it tops
the caprock, cutting through
caliche seams like ice.

A hundred-year-old pew
and a peg to hang your hat
might be your destination,
but the gin's long gone
and speaking of, there never was
a roadhouse or saloon, just one
old country store where someone
still posts handbills on the
unlocked door, the old-school
playground made of cold steel pipe,
a cotton crop unwatered and unpicked,
a rodeo arena, out of use,
no thing the taxman might
remotely tag as new.

Say you needed to reach the capital
by evening, or urgent business
beckoned you to Lubbock,
maybe you should've picked the
four-lane after all. Say you'd
let your GPS guide you astray though,
say you'd wondered what
enchantments lay along the
dim blue line. Or maybe you took
this rambling route for a reason
you didn't even recognize,
and if that option took you
nowhere known to you till now,
my friend, you've chosen well.

The road to Flomot, August 2014

Route 66 westbound from Texola, Oklahoma, 2016

Hundredth Meridian

Rain follows the plow, the nester
pamphlet swore, but that claim
didn't hold water. Wrecked
farmsteads blew away,
Okies trickled west. Next
thing you heard, they'd
deserted by the carload.
Past the chained
and vested line Elk City,
Hydro, Hext, Texola
drove the Mother Road,
hobos rode the rails.
                        Why,
knowing what they knew,
did they not travel east?
At least back home
they'd seen some green.
An exodus, a one-way
track, as though once
trained upon the sun
the wheel couldn't turn:
left of Eden they pressed
on across the plains
to sweat and burn
in so much
dry.

The Bankhead Highway, Eastland, 2021

The rock chip

started
as a sandspur
where the safety glass
collided with a road-flung stone.

So it remained for twenty thousand miles.

Till one hot day it bloomed and spread,
a blade with spikelets striking at the air,
its rhizomes rooted where the wiper met the hood.

I watched the inflorescence slowly grow,

then freeze with unpredicted speed.
It shot into a wicked scythe, a slice
of nothingness dividing nothing clean in half.

Its sickle mowed my field of vision short.

In one last brilliant crack it arced toward earth,
a bow, a graceful seed, airborne,
and paused mid-flight,
                fermata,
                        holding breath

as though the show were not quite over yet:

It's stuck there still, the windshield on the right intact —
the traveler's view as clear as virgin light,
the driver's shattered stars,
the highway indivisible
and infinite and
bright.

Easter Comes to Tom Green County

for Kay

The road's a flat-felled seam of dust stretched taut
    beneath a stone-washed Texas sky. I don't
get out here much these days. *You must
    stay pretty busy with that job back East,*

says B.C., riding shotgun, as the miles
    roll by. From Abilene to Robert Lee
the scene's the same old same old, harrowed fields,
    rusted pumpjacks, barbed-wire, purple sage.

We pass the cattle auction and the lake.
    It rained this March, he says after a spell.
Come a norther, more'n we seen in years.
    The green of the mesquite trees bears him out.

Around the curve the pickup switches gears;
    we're closer to hill country, heading south
across the county line. Not long to go
    before the gathering in San Angelo. And then

    the landscape changes like a trumpet blast:

bluebonnets blanket every rocky slope.
    Man, Dad, you ever see a sight like that?
He thinks about the question. *Nope.* I see the
    tear well up. He brims his Stetson lower,

looks away across the blue
        profusion, daisies sprinkled in like gold.
Dry majesty, thorn-circled, flower-crowned,
        a carpet for a king, these desert hills.

Nobody plants 'em there, you know. The seed's
        just lying in the ground. In times of drought
it waits, he tells me. *It can keep until*
        the rains come. And when they do, at last . . .

    He looks away across the blue.

Lake Colorado City State Park, April 2015

Texas 86, Late October

Who gets to go in gold,
on two-lane grosgrain stitched
across cloud-cottoned canyon?

In luxury of autumn leaves
soft sheets at rooster crow
to ride the black-and-braided

passements of splendent fields,
past range of cattle, deer, and lark—
a path that *was* the past?

Of bison seeking stream and feed,
pursued by flint-armed stalkers,
corona-gilded morions and lances,

horses headed to Cibola's cities,
settlers under Conestoga sail,
the trail of bareback mounted bowmen,

herders, plowmen, soldiers, traders,
with their women, dogs, and young,
chuck wagons, iron horses, horseless

carriages, macadam roads,
their yellow goods to sell,
crop dusters top-dressing low

across the gleaming rows of bolls,
their distant contrails glowing
in the dawn-lit sky?

Who gets to go in gold for miles
on ingots glinting down a center line
past amber diamond highway signs,

a palomino mare, a sycamore,
a spray of chinaberry globes,
hay bales a lady's necklace laid

across a scarf of linen field,
the milo heading out,
the wheat waist-high,

canary-colored harrow
dozing in the straw
and ocher stubble,

half-full school bus
slowing, rumbling by?
Who gets to go in gold?

You'd need to rise in time,
for all of yesterday is overlain
with brick and bone and only

at the early hour shines
like new, like home,
at last.

AGO

Grain elevators, Happy, January 2018

The Finney Gin

still stands,
diminished thing
that once was all
there'd been to call
a siding and a
shipping dock
a stop, a pin-dot
plotted on a
county map;
existing solely
as a spot to
bring in crops,
Finney never won
post office, school,
or census tract.

Still, back when
trucks lined up
from dawn to dark,
delinters, gin stands,
trash bins, oil mills ran
in endless shifts;
trains freighted bales
to market daily.

Then inventions—stripper,
spindle picker, module
builder—did Finney in.
Business dwindled, din
of saws went mum,

dryers' hum spun
to a halt, and
ginners
quit.

Today mute sentinel
of corrugated tin
beside the Santa Fe,
skylights free to pigeons,
skeleton wind-bent
and blooming rust,
it's *gone to seed*,
they'd say, their
metaphor for all
resources left to
their devices,
finished, come to
roost and rest,
standstill.

Cotton gin, Crosbyton, March 2021

Fourteen

Fourteen degrees. He grumbles out of bed;
there's ice to break, there's livestock to be fed.

He zips his Carharrts, cranks the Chevrolet,
heads out to pasture, Thermos under arm.
A golden eagle rises in the east
across the breaks and lights the pickup's way;

against the hues of dawn, arriving geese
glide in to harvest what remains to farm
each season when the strippers leave the wrack
to sandhill cranes, their sere midwinter feast.

He tallies cattle, checks the pasture back
behind the ridge. It's there he stops a while,
gets out his hat and gloves and walks
with last night's ham and biscuit in a sack.

After his lunch, a cold nap in the cab;
then spends his midday hours mending fence
beneath the watchful gaze of red-tailed hawks.
Blue ice on playa lake a solid slab

of diamond, rime of silver on its bank,
the distant revolution of the gins
in January, spinning round the clock,
a windmill hard beside its frozen tank.

The coin of sun soon slips into its slot,
can see to can't, the life he's always led.
How vast the gap between this frost and warm;
how slim the span between have and have not.

Back home he parks the truck, refreshes hay.
There could be poorer ways to spend a day.

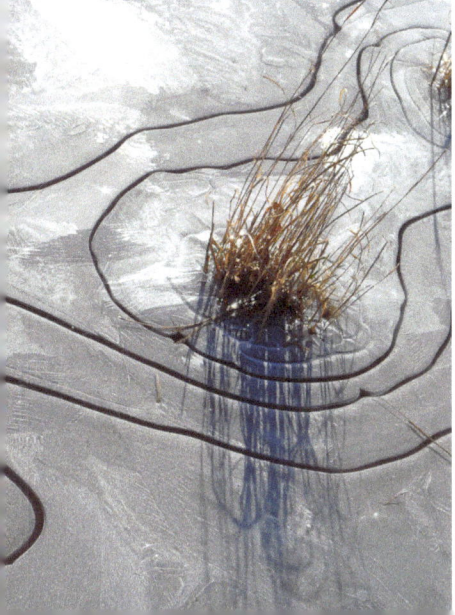

Frozen playa, Lubbock, 2011

Pos

*Paint your p
says the county
Marks your*

If you're an avid back-country explorer or typ
take special care to notice purple trees and fence
from constantly having to replace signs, and t
to even colorblind individuals. So, next time y
or tree, take caution in crossing that
onto someone's p
TEXASHILLCO

*If you me
peekers and p
coming on*

Notice can be in the form of readily vi
and placement on trees or posts sp
on forest land or 1,000 fee
TEXAS PARKS

*a can of sp
provides a cl
warns No T*

It holds the same weight and
EASTTEXASM

*A violet
is an endur
visible*

ted

osts purple,
game warden.
boundaries.

ically find yourself going off the beaten path,
posts. . . . This strategy simply keeps landowners
he color purple was chosen because it is visible
ou spot purple paint in Texas on a fence post
line because you're then venturing
rivate property.
UNTRY.COM

an to stop
oachers from
your land,

sible purple paint marks of proper size
aced no more than 100 feet apart
t apart on non-forest land.
& WILDLIFE

ray paint
ear defense,
respassing.

the same law violations apply.
ATTERS.COM

bruise
ing witness
to all.

Boundary along the Ozark Trail, Tampico, March 2018

Half-mown

the strip remained
beside the barrow ditch
past breakfast time,
the half-mile neighbor saw
and by that evening knew
to dial the phone
and say,
Is everything okay?
Your husband's tractor—

and an answer partly
whimper, partly wail:

The mare was in the barn
and waiting for her feed,
replied the wife,
once she could find
the words.
              She never kicks.

Him only six. My boy—
she did not speak his name—
Mr. Jackson wrapped him
in my coat and laid him
on the truck's
back seat—

           She paused
to gasp another breath

before describing how
they'd almost cheated death,

the father passing ninety
as she grasped an ashen palm
and tried to pray,
the horseshoe mark turned
up for luck but open,
draining life
away

Bassett Farm, Kosse, 2017

Molly Goodnight, savior of the Southern Plains bison, depicted in Veryl Goodnight's "Back from the Brink," Goodnight, Texas, 2014

Assisted Living

When she got too crotchety
for old Harriett to handle,

too many pills and needles
to ration, hips too brittle

to risk a fall, her memory
slipping away like sand,

they had to admit Nana
couldn't stay alone.

I visit her at the home
most Fridays after school.

She wants to make a blanket,
nothing fancy, just a task to

keep her mind off things. I take
the bone hook in my fingers,

demonstrate the stitch: a deft turn
of the wrist, dip left, back up,

catch the lasso, pull it through.
Repeat. The shell takes shape.

I hold her bird's-foot twigs
of hands within the nest

of mine, the way she did when
I was ten and she taught me

the trick. Nana talks to her designs.
I listen. When the yarn runs out

the pattern of the rows has gone
all wrong: a twisted maze of

loops and clusters, mismatched
DNA. It's not the details

she forgets, only the way
they're strung together, just what

order they should take. So when
she dozes off and lets the chain

drop from her grasp, I gently pull
the frazzled skein, unravel

back to where it fell apart
so we can start again another day

State Fair of Texas, 2017

AWAY

Courthouse floor, Brownsville, February 2018

Azulejos
At the State Fair

My job, to mop.
Cada hora.
Gray lines between glazed tiles
grow grayer as the soles of ghosts
track in and out of metal stalls,
straight rows between tiled walls.

Wear smock, punch clock.
Todo el día.
Take mop and pail, unlock
the door. The lines line up.
I find my spot beside the sink.
In here there is no clock to watch.

Wet floor, mop more.
Piso mojado.
Dirty shoes on grout go out, go in.
I know their boots and sandals.
In a haze I count the squares
like days laid on the sheet of months.

Hill County, en route to Junction

Sextet
Junction, one May

We're here for Tech's
most promising
and fertile minds,
to get a peek
at all their most
inventive lines.

The word is sex,
the force of nature
through the fuse
of flowers quick
to apprehend
the latest news.

Under the oaks
they stand to read.
How can we hear
the poets' work
amid the running
of the deer?

Prepare

Set holy bones
of your name saint
within a niche
beside the door.

Bake sweet and spice
into a cake
as succor for
the starving poor.

Dig a turnip
from your garden,
carve a lantern,
then take care:

Do not be caught
this eve without
a light, an alms,
a hallow's prayer.

Herd in pasture, Happy, February 2016

Evicted

At least we waited till the young had fledged.
Their mud nest occupied a porch-roof ledge
above the door. You knew to wear a hat.
You dodged fresh droppings on the welcome mat.

That virus year, we let the swallows stay;
the lake house went unrented anyway,
and while few human tenants traveled much,
postponement of removal seemed as just.

But in mid-spring when little birds were seen
in practice flight, we had to intervene
before the feral tabby playing dumb
might find her chance. Their checkout time had come.

Not knowing how in bird-speak to convey
their lease was up, and lacking any way
to signify all squatters had to go,
we trained our glasses on the bungalow.

Search "Relocating swallows" and you'll learn
the birds will migrate when the seasons turn.
Sure enough, in June, the avians moved on.
Southward, on vacation, they were gone.

We pried their feather-furnished structure loose,
Scrubbed mud foundations free of further use,
Erased all trace of home against return.
Their future plight was none of our concern.

The Covid moratoriums expired
that summer, too; rent once again required,
evictions recommenced. Whole families
relinquished precious claims to roof and keys.

In other news, more ethnic exiles found
themselves dislodged and sleeping on the ground.
In every place a dwelling is destroyed
another clan swoops in to fill the void.

So it has been, so still will be, this race
among us breeding species seeking space
to call a habitation: roam and rout
and settle, pushing on and pushing out.

Agave Cottage, Spur, July 2022

J. B. Buchanan Windmill Collection, Spearman, 2016

ABOVE

Got to Find a Way Back Down
For Susan and Daron

They called me on the telephone
Said, are you sitting down
You know that condo building,
that old tower south of town

Thirteen plus one unlucky one
Her music broken on the ground
And I knew in that moment
She had to find a way back down,
She's got to find a way back down.

I read it in the paper, babe
I saw it on the news
You played a game of circumstance
You couldn't help but lose

You made it to the big time but
The big time beat you down
I told myself he's flown too high,
He had to find a way back down,
He's got to find a way back down.

No one can catch a falling star
They blaze and fade, that's how they are
It's always earthward they are bound,
They've got to find their way back down,
They've got to find their way back down.

A bridge above a river
No way out but down
Once you've finally figured out
It's better die than drown

They'll say it was the easy way
To leave this sorry town,
Your friends won't understand you,
You had to find your way back down,
You've got to find a way back down.

Skyrockets in a summer sky
A meteor to ground
Descending from the stratosphere
They find their way back down;

And I can hear the melody,
That melancholy sound
A sweet guitar, a rose, a star,
They've got to find their way back down,
They've got to find a way back down.

No one can catch a falling star
They blaze and fade, that's how they are
It's always earthward they are bound,
They've got to find their way back down,
They've got to find their way back down.

A penny on tails, and no one to give it to

By chance, head low,
you might well come upon one-
cent pieces dropped on sidewalks,
left on restaurant floors,
unclaimed in stores.

Some pennies gleam right up
at you with hopeful face.
Grandma says you place
these in your purse
for luck.

But what of others,
profile turned to pavement,
fortune spurned—
Abe gazing down
in dirt?

Tradition has it
you must hand these over
to somebody else,
else bad luck's
yours to keep.

I pocketed one
yesterday. To hang
onto it seemed wrong.
But who's to set a deadline
for passing it along?

When I discover who
I'm meant to give it to,
I guess I'll know.
Until such day I wait,
my property

a single copper
soon to be
bestowed upon
one golden soul
with just the right wish.

Sidewalk, Marfa, December 2021

Interstate 40 Rest Area, westbound, Gray County, 2015

A Wish

May no ill befall you greater than your strength to cope,
 No hardness harsher than ability to care,
 No grief more bitter than capacity for hope;

May no boon arrive beyond your willingness to share.

Bad Blessings

give thanks, give thanks for
adverse experiences,
contrary events

This was no accident. You strode, steadfast and slow, out of boundary berm onto blacktop, indiscernible against autumn remnants of sprawling screwbean. Your hide undivided from camouflaging brush until brakes were past deploy, you kept coming, deliberate, hoof by hoof, even as wheels swerved. As one with the fatal fender, you met your end. The car would never run again.

time-honored Honda
laid to rest a total loss,
we share rides, pay debts

And when your kin crossed our other car days later on a rain-slicked Texas two-lane, souls were spared, though not the yearling deer's. A wakeup call, some say, a blessing in disguise. We hold instead that fate's a coward's cover, happenstance an equal game of chance. Misfortunes spell a counter turn of happy luck, believed the Greeks, for someone else if not for you. Whatever Tyche divines for us, we'll take it: we live, we choose what tale to make of it.

along random roads
damage done, benediction,
worse disaster dodged

Ruins of Harold Dow Bugbee mural, Tascosa Room, Amarillo, 2015

Runway, Spaceport USA, Sierra County, New Mexico, 2014

Last and Final

Deborah Davis to Dallas–Fort Worth,
This is your final boarding call:
Report to Gate 6A at once
Lest you not fly at all.

Miss Davis, see us at the gate:
You do not want to miss
Your flight. Do not be late. This is
Your last and final boarding call.

What is a poem
but a puzzle in the frame
of its own making?

Bassett Farm, Kosse, 2017

This book was set in the Adobe Jenson Pro family of typefaces in
Adobe InDesign. If the spread constitutes the essential unit of book design,
in this volume many two-page poems start on the verso for seamless reading.
Page numbers are likewise often left unsupressed, contrary to convention.
The ministrations of the Ad Hoc Writers of Lubbock have been
invaluable in the shaping of this work over more than a decade.

www.ingramcontent.com/pod-product-compliance
Lightning Source LLC
Chambersburg PA
CBHW042102120526
44592CB00027B/91